Little Dilly Doo
and Lilly Frog Too

PAGE PUBLISHING
Conneaut Lake, PA

First originally published by Page Publishing 2024

ISBN 979-8-89315-870-0 (pbk)
ISBN 979-8-89315-881-6 (digital)

Printed in the United States of America

Little Dilly Doo and Lilly Frog Too

Missy Wilder

Just the other day, Little Dilly Doo was on his way, skipping along and whistling a song when he came across a frog sitting on a log.

She too was whistling a tune when Little
Dilly asked, "Do you have any room?"
Lilly Frog kept on whistling while the
others kept on listening.

Dilly Doo sat on the log next to Lilly the Frog.
Now both were whistling a tune when Timmy
the Turtle came along whistling a song
and asked, "Do you have any room?"

He crawled onto the log next to Lilly the Frog. Now all three were whistling together when two with feathers came along, and they too were whistling a song.

It was nearly noon when they asked,
"Do you have any room?"

The two perched on the log next to Lilly the Frog.

Now all five were whistling a song while
rabbit and squirrel were dancing along.

All seven friends were having fun whistling
and dancing under the sun, but the day is
nearly gone so they must end their song.

"Thank you, Lilly Frog, for making room on your log."

Lilly replied with a croak and a grin, "I always make room for new and old friends."

About the Author

Missy Wilder is happily married and has two sons, a stepdaughter, and one granddaughter. She works full time at Lowe's as an MST. She loves animals and flowers. She also loves working in their woodshop, building and creating things.